Original title:
Christmas Love and Joyful Songs

Copyright © 2024 Creative Arts Management OÜ
All rights reserved.

Author: Nora Sinclair
ISBN HARDBACK: 978-9916-90-972-0
ISBN PAPERBACK: 978-9916-90-973-7

Wrapped in Wool and Wonder

A sheep once took a grand old trip,
She learned that wool could give a rip.
With every stitch, a tale was spun,
And cozy sweaters made it fun.

But one day, oh! What a sight,
A llama joined, and took a bite.
Now scarves have llamas wrapped in glee,
Creating quite the fashion spree!

The Gift of Togetherness

We stuffed our stockings, nice and tight,
With socks instead of gifts, what a sight!
Then Uncle Joe, drank all the cheer,
And danced like he forgot his rear!

Together we laughed, and we would fumble,
Falling in piles, oh how we tumbled!
The gift of togetherness, we found,
Is best when you're rolling on the ground!

Harmonies Beneath the Silver Moon

Under the moon, the frogs did croak,
Their serenade was no joke.
A cat thought it was quite the show,
And joined in with a charming 'meow!'

The owls hooted with rhythm fine,
While squirrels chattered, feeling divine.
The harmony made us all align,
In nature's concert, so divine!

Snowflakes and Sweet Serenades

Snowflakes danced, a thrilling race,
And landed right on grandma's face.
She laughed and slipped, oh what a scene!
The neighbors cheered, a winter queen!

With cocoa cups and cookies near,
We sang our carols, loud and clear.
But when we hit the high notes loud,
The dogs howled back, quite proud!

Sleigh Bells Ringing with Delight

Sleigh bells ringing, oh what fun,
Riding through the snow, we can't outrun.
With reindeer prancing, hooves a-clop,
Santa's on the roof, let's hope he won't drop!

Cookies on the table, milk in a cup,
Imagine his surprise when he sees the pup!
He'll wiggle and giggle, all filled with cheer,
Hope he won't eat the cat, oh dear oh dear!

Snowmen grinning with sticks for arms,
But watch out, they're sly with all their charms.
One blink and they may just come alive,
Maybe they'll dance, and jive, and dive!

So grab your cocoa, let's toast with glee,
To sleigh bells ringing, come and join me.
Let's laugh and be merry, spread joy all around,
In this winter wonderland, pure happiness found!

Fresh Sprouts of Joy and Wonder

Fresh sprouts growing in my tiny pot,
They peek from the dirt, oh what a lot!
They wave their leaves, show their bright green,
Such lively fellows, the best I've seen!

I water them gently, give them some sun,
Tell them funny jokes, oh how they run!
They giggle and wiggle, sprouting with glee,
Maybe they'll grow up to be a big tree!

A plant with a hat, oh what a view,
With shades on its leaves, absolutely true!
Playing hide and seek with the curious cat,
They're quite the duo, imagine that!

So let's plant some joy, and sprinkle some love,
These sprouts of wonder fit like a glove.
In the garden of laughter, we'll dance and sway,
With fresh joy blooming, come join the play!

Whispers of the Winter Heart

Snowflakes fell with a flourish,
Yet I lost my car in the slush.
I danced like a penguin in glee,
But my boots said, 'Let's just flee.'

Hot cocoa spills on the floor,
As I trip and crash through the door.
My cat, in skis, takes a dive,
I guess winter's a party to survive!

Melodies Beneath the Mistletoe

Under the mistletoe, I trip,
Spilled a drink on my date's lip.
They laughed, not offended a bit,
"Let's dance; we'll call it a hit!"

My Aunt's sweater's a sight to behold,
It jingles and sparkles, full of bold.
We sing carols off-key, what a show,
Who needs talent, with love in tow?

Frosted Dreams of Togetherness

Building a snowman, oh what a treat,
But he's now a pile of melted defeat.
We tried to give him a top hat, you see,
But the dog thought he looked like a snack, yum spree!

In my dreams, it's a winter wonder,
Until I wake to hear the thunder.
The sled rides turn into a race,
With my brother, it's no longer grace!

Radiant Nights and Starry Lights

We lit up the house like a beacon,
Neighbors think we're lost in a weekend.
The twinkling lights flash with flair,
As my cat turns into a festive bear.

The glue for crafts stuck my fingers tight,
Now my glitter shines brighter at night.
Family gatherings, oh what a cheer,
If chaos is festive, we lead the sphere!

The Gift of Laughter in the Snow

Snowflakes fall with a laugh,
Kids bundled up like marshmallows.
They tumble down with joy,
In a snowball fight that glows.

Parents sip cocoa, eyes aglow,
As laughter echoes in the breeze.
With each throw, faces in snow,
The winter chill brought to its knees.

Embrace Under the Evergreen

Under the tree, they snicker and sway,
Dancing like ornaments, bright and gay.
Lights twinkle with delight,
As they stumble through the night.

"Watch your step!" someone shouts with glee,
While one trips over a rogue pine tree.
Laughter rings through the air,
Joy found everywhere.

Harmonies in the Silent Night

Silent night, the cats are yowling,
In tune with the stars, so astoundingly.
Dogs howl back, with all their might,
A serenade under the moonlight.

Chimneys puff out festive smoke,
Neighbors gather, sharing a joke.
Around the fire, we chuckle and cheer,
Celebrating life with friends near.

Warmth in the Chill of December

December's chill crunches our toes,
But hot soup brings warmth, as everyone knows.
We sip and we slurp, our faces aglow,
Sharing stories of winter's good show.

Mittens mismatched, and hats askew,
Snowball aims that just won't do.
In the frosty air, laughter breeds cheer,
December's warmth is finally here!

A Dance Among Evergreen Hues

In the forest where trees do sway,
Squirrels gossip and dance all day.
Mice wear shoes made of shiny bark,
And twirl around till it gets dark.

Frogs croak tunes in a vibrant choir,
While a beetle plays on a string of wire.
The woodpecker joins with a tap and a clop,
And all the creatures just can't stop.

They shuffle left and they shimmy right,
Twirling around in the pale moonlight.
A raccoon leads with a big ol' grin,
Saying, "Come on now, let the fun begin!"

So join this dance, don't be a bore,
Swing with the trees, let your spirit soar.
With evergreen hues and laughter so bright,
Let's dance till dawn, what a magical sight!

Radiant Moments Wrapped in Cheer

A sunbeam tickles a sleepy cat,
Who jumps up startled, now imagine that!
With silly poses, it prances around,
Chasing its tail, oh what a sound!

In the kitchen, cookies pop and bake,
While the dog dreams of a giant steak.
Kids giggle as flour flies up high,
Creating a cloud that floats to the sky.

A rainbow sprinkles laughter on toast,
And makes silly faces that we love most.
Mom's secret recipe facial cream,
Is nothing but whipped cream—they all scream!

With radiant moments as sweet as pie,
Wrap up the joy, let the giggles fly.
So raise a glass to cheer and jest,
In this funny life, we are truly blessed!

Frosty Kisses and Sweet Reunions

Snowflakes dance down, like tiny hugs,
While snowmen sport their carrot mugs.
Frosty kisses on cheeks so bright,
In a world turned sparkling white.

With mittens tucked, we build and slide,
Squeals of laughter, a winter ride.
The dog leaps high, with a joyful bark,
Chasing snowballs till it's dark.

Hot cocoa waits, marshmallows afloat,
As we warm up by the fire's note.
Stories shared, with laughter, we chat,
While the kitten snoozes on grandma's hat.

In sweet reunions with hugs from friends,
We cheer to winter that never ends.
With frosty kisses, let laughter reign,
In warm hearts, it's all worth the gain!

Twinkling Stars and Gentle Smiles

Under the sky where twinkling stars,
Wish for candy and shiny cars.
The moon winks down with a gleeful cheer,
While crickets play their songs so dear.

Bunnies hop with a magical grace,
Losing their carrots in a playful race.
Fireflies join in, lighting up the night,
Creating a dance that feels just right.

Gentle smiles bloom like flowers in spring,
As we gather round to laugh and sing.
With snacks of popcorn and fizzy drinks,
We share our secrets while the world winks.

So let's gaze up and enjoy the show,
With twinkling stars, let our dreams grow.
In moments of joy, we can embrace,
The magic of night in this blissful space!

Lanterns Lighting Up Kindred Souls

In the night, the lanterns glow,
Bringing laughter, to and fro.
They dance around like little sprites,
Guiding us on these playful nights.

With jingling bells and silly hats,
We'll share our joy with singing cats.
The shadows giggle, the moonlight grins,
In this dance, everyone's a win!

Friends gather 'round with stories bold,
Of secret treasures and tales untold.
As lanterns sway and shadows prance,
We find our rhythm, we find our dance.

So lift your glass and raise a cheer,
For kindred souls who gather near.
With twinkling lights and hearts so free,
We'll light the night in harmony!

The Spirit That Wraps Around Us

With a blanket of giggles, we snuggle tight,
The spirit surrounds us, what a silly sight!
The cat joins in with a purring cheer,
As we share our stories, loud and clear.

A ghost in the corner, with a lopsided grin,
Challenges us to a silly spin.
We'll twirl and twist, let the spirit guide,
In this joyous chaos, none can hide.

With laughter weaving through the air,
Every ghostly friend makes us aware:
That the spirit that wraps is all about fun,
Making us laugh until we can't run!

So here's to the night, to the giggles we share,
To the friends that surround, showing love and care.
Wrap me up tight in this humorous spree,
The spirit that binds us, just let it be!

Enchanted Nights and Whimsical Hearts

In enchanted nights, where dreams take flight,
Whimsical hearts dance with pure delight.
A jester's cap, a playful spin,
Let's laugh together, let the fun begin!

With starlit skies and fairies bold,
We chase our dreams, let the night unfold.
In every twinkle, a giggle's found,
With whimsical hearts, our joy knows no bounds.

A talking tree joins our merry play,
Cracking jokes in the grand ballet.
His bark is worse than his funny bit,
He tells us tales where we all fit!

So let's embrace the magical air,
With enchanted nights, we shall declare:
That laughter is key to whimsical hearts,
In this world of wonder, joy never departs!

Glee in the Dazzling Chill

In the dazzling chill, we bundle tight,
With scarves and mittens, what a sight!
Snowflakes fall like confetti bright,
We twirl and tumble, pure delight!

With frosty noses and cheeks so red,
We launch our snowballs, bouncing instead.
Laughter erupts, it fills the air,
In the chilly glee, we shed our care.

Fireside stories, marshmallows roast,
Our silly antics, we love the most.
With cocoa smiles and hearts aglow,
In the winter magic, we steal the show!

So here's to the chill that makes us sing,
To joyful moments that winter can bring.
With gleeful spirits, we'll make a thrill,
In this dazzling chill, we chase our fill!

Under the Mistletoe's Glow

Under the mistletoe, I stand still,
Waiting for my kiss, against my will.
But my cat leaps in, what a sight,
Now I'm in trouble, no love tonight!

A friend walks by, I try to peek,
He catches me grinning, oh so sleek.
"Is that your date?" he cracks a cheer,
I salute the cat, my furry dear!

With one tiny meow, he steals the show,
Who knew beneath mistletoe, love can grow?
Next year I vow, no cat in sight,
Just me and my plans to kiss tonight!

So here's to moments, silly and bright,
Under the mistletoe, laughter takes flight.
Let's raise our glasses, and give a cheer,
For furry distractions, this time of year!

Tinsel Dreams and Laughter

Tinsel dreams are shining bright,
Twinkling well into the night.
But the cat thinks it's a toy,
Wreaking havoc, oh what joy!

Decorations hang, all aglow,
Then the dog comes, moving slow.
They chase the light, with all their might,
Creating chaos, what a sight!

The cookies baked, they smell divine,
But then the sneaky pup does dine.
With crumbs and laughter, we recall,
Next year we'll hide them up the hall!

In this house of joy, mess, and cheer,
We gather 'round, the ones most dear.
With tinsel dreams and laughter's spark,
Our holidays shine, even in the dark!

Warmth Beneath the Starry Skies

Beneath the stars, in winter's chill,
We huddle close, it's quite the thrill.
But where's my hat? I shout in vain,
"Oh look, a squirrel!" waits to explain.

Marshmallows dance on sticks of wood,
While we sip cocoa, all feel good.
A snowball flies, I duck and sway,
Only to hear laughter, "Merry play!"

The fire crackles, oh how it glows,
But wait, my shoes are lost in snow!
With giggles echoing through the night,
It's just a party beneath moonlight.

So let's embrace this silly scene,
With warmth and smiles, all in between.
Under the stars, with laughter's rise,
We find our joys beneath the skies!

Bright Lights and Cherished Hearts

Bright lights twinkle on the street,
But watch your step, don't miss a beat.
Falling snowflakes, soft and white,
Then slip—oh dear!—a comical sight!

Carols sung in voices loud,
So off-key, it forms a crowd.
"Oh what fun!" we all do cheer,
As the dog joins in, without a fear!

With cherished hearts and merry snacks,
We gather 'round, no thoughts of lacks.
The turkey's burnt, the pie's a flop,
But laughter shared, we'll never stop!

So here's to love, and silly glee,
With bright lights and friends, we're full of spree.
Let's hold each other, not fall apart,
For holidays shine with cherished hearts!

A Festive Tangle of Hearts

In the kitchen, pots collide,
Cookies dancing, can't decide.
The flour's flying, what a sight,
Sugar rush till late tonight.

Tinsel hangs from every door,
Cats are tangled, can't ignore.
Grandma's knitting in a knot,
Sweater styles we forgot what!

Presents piled, a sight to see,
Wrapped with love, and chaos, whee!
Uncle Joe's loud laughter roars,
Knocking over all the floors.

With each cheer and silly game,
Heartfelt joy is just the same.
In this tangle, laughter starts,
Holidays wrap around our hearts.

The Glow of Togetherness

Lights are twinkling on the tree,
Grandpa's snoring, oh so free.
A blanket fort, we call our home,
With snack attack, we freely roam.

Sipping cocoa with a grin,
Marshmallows have been declared a win.
In our jammies, cozy bliss,
This sweet moment we won't miss.

A game of charades never ends,
Falling over, we're all friends.
With silly jokes that always land,
It's joy wrapped in a little band.

Together here, we shine so bright,
Turning chaos into light.
In this glow, love truly speaks,
Filling up our hearts for weeks.

Melodies on a Snowy Evening

Snowflakes falling, soft and fine,
Whispers of winter, oh so divine.
Sleds are flying, laughter rings,
Who knew snow could sprout such swings?

Hot cocoa brews, marshmallows dive,
Dad sings poorly, but we thrive.
Chasing snowmen across the yard,
Every snowball thrown hits hard!

The radio plays our favorite song,
We join in, all sing along.
With hearts so light, we'll dance and sway,
In the snow, we'll laugh and play.

As the stars twinkle bright above,
This evening wraps us in warm love.
With melodies that fill the night,
Snowy evenings bring pure delight.

Sweeter Than Any Sugarplum

Cookies lined up, a glorious sight,
Frosting battles, who'll take the bite?
Jingle bells ring, we taste and laugh,
Sugar high? We're just on half!

Candy canes, a colorful swarm,
Sticky fingers take the norm.
In the kitchen, chaos reigns,
Cookie dough flying like small trains!

Silly faces in icing grace,
Decorating with our own style pace.
A sprinkle here, a dab of glee,
Who knew baking could bring such glee?

With every nibble, love does swell,
These sweet creations cast a spell.
Sweeter than plums, our giggling fun,
In this joyful bake-off, we've all won!

Sledding Down Memory Lane

Racing down the hill so steep,
With hot cocoa that makes you leap.
Our sleds are flying, oh what a ride,
But wait! There's a snowman we just can't hide!

Crunching snow beneath our boots,
We giggle loud, pulling funny hoots.
Fell flat on our faces, oh what a sight,
Yet, we can't stop laughing, it feels just right!

A snowball fight ensues with flair,
Dodging and weaving everywhere.
Old man Johnson's porch is now a zone,
Of furry snowballs he won't condone!

When we're finally home, drenched to the core,
Mum shakes her head; we just want more.
Sledding memories, they freeze like ice,
Forever our laughable, cherished slice!

Glittering Stars and Glistening Snow

Stars twinkle bright in the winter night,
As snowflakes twirl, oh what a sight!
Building dreams in the frosty air,
With marshmallows dancing without a care.

Hot chocolate spills, oh what a mess,
Whipped cream towers, quite the finesse!
Slipping and sliding on ice so slick,
Each fall is magical, really quite the trick!

We toss snowballs like skilled little pros,
But right in the face, my brother it goes!
He dives in the snow, all flustered in pride,
While we're still laughing, he tries to hide.

As evening falls, we'll snuggle real tight,
Sharing stories of stars shining bright.
Glittering stars and snowflakes aglow,
In the warmth of our hearts, winter's magic will flow!

A Tapestry of Warmth and Wonder

In a cozy corner, we gather 'round,
With tales of old that joyously sound.
Blankets piled high as we sip and share,
A tapestry woven with love and care.

Grandma's cookies smell like blessed dreams,
Chocolate chip and nutty themes.
We munch and chat, the smiles unfold,
Looks like we'd rather stay young than grow old!

Outside it's chilly, but in here we glow,
Creating our stories, all wrapped in flow.
With a wink and a laugh, our troubles grow small,
Together in warmth, we can conquer it all!

So let the snow fall, let winter arrive,
In this tapestry of warmth, we thrive.
Together we journey, through laughter and cheer,
In the fabric of wonder, we hold so dear.

Together Through the Winter's Tale

Together we venture through winter's tale,
With frosty breaths that trail like a snail.
Sleds packed and ready for escapades grand,
Bound for adventure, just hand in hand.

Snowflakes whirl like a swirling dance,
We'll capture them all if given a chance!
A snow fort built with walls so high,
Defending our kingdom, oh me, oh my!

We share big laughs as we tumble and roll,
Making snow angels, it's good for the soul.
A flash in the air, then snowballs unleashed,
A wintertime battle, all served as a feast!

As stars twinkle over our cold, frozen land,
With cheeks rosy red, we still understand.
That together forever, through thick and through thin,
In this winter's tale, we always win!

Hearts Adrift on Winter Winds

Snowflakes fall like tiny socks,
While snowmen steal the neighbor's rocks.
Hot chocolate flows, marshmallows dive,
In this land where we all thrive.

Icicles hang like frozen spears,
Frosty air brings out our cheers.
We bundle up, say 'cozy mate',
But forget the key—oh, what a fate!

Mittens lost and toes that freeze,
Winter's charm is sure to tease.
We laugh and slip, oh what a sight,
As we twirl through the snowy night.

Though hearts may drift like icebergs stray,
We'll warm them up with fun and play.
With each chuckle, our worries cease,
In winter folly, we find our peace.

Luminous Nights and Kindred Spirits

Stars twinkle like a disco ball,
While friends stand tall, ready to call.
The moon whispers secrets in the breeze,
As laughter dances among the trees.

Kindred spirits sip their wine,
Telling tales that twist and entwine.
Flashlights flicker, shadows prance,
Under the sky, we love to dance.

Marshmallows roast on sticks that bend,
While we tease and joke, we all ascend.
Fireflies twinkle like our delight,
In luminous nights, everything feels right.

So let us cherish these moments rare,
With kindred souls who truly care.
As laughter echoes in the night,
We find our way by friendship's light.

Voices Rise in Joyful Harmony

Singing off-key, we raise our glass,
While neighbors wonder what the heck? We skip on beat,
just like a frog,
And make our own sweet symphonic fog.

With spoons for drums and pots in hand,
Our joyful noise is simply grand.
We harmonize with laughter bright,
Creating music in pure delight.

Choruses formed of silly dreams,
As we bumble through our loud extremes.
Each voice a note in our wild symphony,
Creating chaos, yet feeling free.

So join our jolly cacophony here,
In joyful harmony, we persevere.
With every note, our spirits soar,
What a magical melody, who could ask for more?

The Joyful Parade of Warm Reflections

A parade of socks, mismatched delight,
Wobbling through the sunny light.
With hats too big and smiles too wide,
We march along, filled with pride.

Teddies wave from off the float,
As we sing songs that just won't gloat.
Candy rain falls from the sky,
Look out, it's sweet and oh so spry!

Balloons fly high like dreams unchained,
While funny faces keep us entertained.
Giggles tumble and joy ignites,
In this parade of pure delights.

So hold my hand, let's march along,
In this joyful parade, where we belong.
With warm reflections, we'll conquer the day,
And dance through life in our silly way.

The Dance of Joyful Spirits

In the town square, spirits twirl,
With goofy moves that make us hurl.
They shimmy and shake, they leap so high,
Leaving giggles and snorts as they fly.

Their socks mismatched, shoes untied,
They dance with glee, and never hide.
Twirling 'round like tops in a spin,
Laughing out loud: 'Let the fun begin!'

Under moonlight, they spin and sway,
Tripping on toes in a comical way.
Joyful spirits, let's join the fun,
With silly dances, we're never done!

So if you feel blue, and need a lift,
Jump in the fray, it's the perfect gift.
With joy in our hearts, we'll laugh and play,
In the dance of spirits, we'll brighten the day!

Sipping Cocoa, Sharing Dreams

With mugs in hand, we sit and sip,
Hot cocoa smiles, that's the best trip.
Marshmallows bob, like boats at sea,
Together we dream, just you and me.

The steam curls up like a whispered wish,
As visions arise, oh, what a dish!
A world of candy, where laughter reigns,
With chocolate rivers and gumdrop plains.

We giggle and chatter, our spirits bright,
With each silly hope, we take flight.
From castles made of marshmallow fluff,
To unicorns dancing, it's all just enough.

So raise your mug, let's toast with cheer,
For in cocoa dreams, there's nothing to fear.
With each creamy sip, our cares drift away,
Sipping cocoa together, forever we'll stay!

Sweet Whispers of Hope and Cheer

In a garden where daisies bloom,
Whispers of hope make a bright room.
With petals soft as a child's hug,
Cheerful wishes give life a tug.

The sun peeks in with a warm embrace,
While laughter dances at a lively pace.
A breeze carries tales, both old and new,
Igniting our hearts with a lovely view.

With every whisper, we plant a seed,
Of cheer and joy, it's all we need.
Let's sprinkle love like confetti bright,
In this cheerful realm, everything's right.

So hold my hand, let's skip with glee,
Through sweet whispers of what could be.
In this garden of dreams, we freely roam,
With laughter and love, we'll find our home!

The Promise of Togetherness

In a cozy nook, we gather near,
To share our giggles, spread the cheer.
With silly stories and cookies to munch,
Every moment together is a joyful punch.

We build our castles with pillows and dreams,
With laughter echoing, or so it seems.
Fortresses strong made of giggles and hugs,
Surrounded by warmth, with cozy snug bugs.

Out in the world, life can feel gray,
But together we chase all the clouds away.
With the promise of friendship, so shiny and bright,
We'll frolic through life, hearts taking flight.

So here's to us, in this lovely spree,
For every adventure, just you and me.
With the promise of togetherness shining clear,
We'll conquer the world, spreading joy and cheer!

Songs from the Heart's Hearth

In the kitchen, pots do sing,
Spaghetti's twirling, it's quite the fling.
With sauce smeared across my cheek,
I lip-sync to the tunes I seek.

The oven's baking crisp and warm,
Yet somehow, a cookie's gone, that charm.
I dance like no one's watching me,
Except the cat who disagrees.

Pizza dough flies across the floor,
My dinner's now a circus score.
I juggle lettuce, can't you see?
Cooking's just a comedy.

When friends arrive, the laughter grows,
With spilled drinks and various woes.
We toast our hearts to kitchen art,
As I sing songs from my heart's hearth.

Celebrations Under the Silver Moon

Underneath the silver light,
We tried to fly a kite at night.
But it got stuck up in a tree,
A party foul, oh woe is me!

The cake was shaped like a big shoe,
We all agreed it was so blue.
With frosting fights and silly grins,
We licked our fingers, blessed our sins.

A piñata swung, all eyes aglow,
Out tumbled candy, a glorious show.
But in the frenzy, someone fell,
And grabbed a handful - oh what the hell!

So here's to laughs beneath the sky,
Where even a mishap can make us high.
With every cheer and silly tune,
We celebrate beneath the moon.

Radiance Wrapped in Holiday Cheer

Lights are twinkling, looking bright,
But someone tangled them up tight.
Now they blink like disco balls,
The cat just stares, he's seen it all.

The cookies burned, oh dear, oh my,
We laughed till we almost cried.
With frosting that looked like a mess,
Desperate times, we did our best!

The tree is lopsided, taken aback,
It leans to one side, what a knack.
But every ornament tells a tale,
As we sip our eggnog without fail.

So gather 'round, let laughter ring,
With joy and cheer, together we sing.
In chaos we find our holiday cheer,
Wrapped in love, we hold each other near.

Love Letters in the Snowflakes

Snowflakes fell like whispered dreams,
I wrote you love notes, or so it seems.
But every word turned into a flake,
Then fluttered off - what a mistake!

I tried to carve your name in the snow,
But slipped on ice, oh no, oh no!
Instead of hearts, I drew a mess,
Now passersby just laugh, I guess.

The mailbox filled with winter's air,
With letters stuck, my woes laid bare.
But every time I try to send,
The winter chill, my only friend.

So here's my love, a frosty note,
With snowflakes dancing as I wrote.
Though ink may fade and paper flee,
My heart's the letter, can't you see?

Whirling Snowflakes and Joyful Rhymes

Snowflakes twirl like ballerinas,
Dancing down from sky to ground.
They freeze my nose and tickle my toes,
Get ready for snowball fights abound!

Hot cocoa spills, a marshmallow flood,
The floor's a lake, oh what a mess!
We laugh and slip in a chocolate-smudge,
Who knew that winter's such a stress?

Sledding down the neighbor's hill,
We race like crazy, no fear at all.
But as we tumble, it's quite a thrill,
I love the sound of the snowball's call!

With every flake, the fun ignites,
We build a snowman, tall and spry.
He wears a hat and two coal eyes,
Look out! He's watching! Oh my, oh my!

Harmonies of a Starlit Night

Beneath the stars, we sing and sway,
My cat joins in, what a serenade!
He hits the high notes in his own way,
Meow-sic magic in the moonlit glade!

We strum a tune on ketchup bottles,
And dance like penguins, round and round.
With laundry on our heads, oh what models,
The best-dressed stars in our own sound!

The night is young, laughter flies,
We spot a comet, it zooms so bright.
With each little wish, we touch the skies,
Harmonies of a starlit night!

So grab your friends and hum along,
In this crazy world, we'll all be wrong.
No notes to follow, just joyous song,
Life is simple when we belt out strong!

Every Heart a Christmas Tree

Every heart's a Christmas tree,
Decked in love and funny cheer.
Some are bright and some are wild,
With a touch of glitter, oh so dear!

Lights that twinkle, hugs that shine,
Decorate with laughter and jokes.
Santa's sleigh just dropped a line,
Delivering joy to all the folks!

Cookies, sweets, and laughter flow,
As family gathers, tales unfold.
A bit too much eggnog, oh no!
But who cares? We're all feeling bold!

So raise a glass, let's toast and cheer,
To every heart that's bright and free.
May every day feel like this year—
A joyful dance 'neath every tree!

The Cozy Chorus of Togetherness

Gather 'round, it's time to feast,
With grandma's pie and dad's strange dance.
The dog joins in, a hungry beast,
Snatching crumbs, oh what a chance!

We share our hugs and jokes galore,
Like silly geese, we flap and flap.
Laughing until our bellies sore,
Togetherness is a comfy wrap!

The fire crackles, stories flow,
We reminisce on times we've been.
With each wild tale, our hearts aglow,
In this cozy chorus, we win!

So here's to love, family cheers,
To every giggle, every grin.
These moments are the best souvenirs,
In the cozy chorus, we all tune in!

Lullabies of the Hearth

The cat's on the rug, in a deep, silly dream,
Chasing after mice, or so it would seem.
The dog snorts a note, like a trumpet in flight,
Sleepy giggles echo, into the soft night.

The kettle's in battle, it whistles and screams,
While Dad tries to soothe it with sweet, sleepy themes.
Mom's in the kitchen, tossing in more spice,
"Just one more cookie!" I said—oh, how nice!

The blanket's a fortress, the pillows a hill,
Tangled in laughter, we snuggle until.
Each little snore, a lullaby's tune,
As dreams dance around us, beneath the bright moon.

So drift off, dear hearts, let the hearth be your guide,
With giggles and warmth, we'll snuggle inside.
In this comical chaos, we find our sweet rest,
In the lullabies sung, we're forever so blessed.

Joyful Hearts Around the Fire

Gathered 'round the fire, the marshmallows toast,
Stories of monsters, we love them the most.
S'mores are a battle, they melt and they drip,
With sticky, sweet giggles, we gobble a bit!

Uncle Joe tells a tale, one tall as a tree,
Of the time he danced with a great bumblebee.
We laugh 'til we cry, our sides all in pain,
As fireflies join in, a shimmering train.

A game of charades, Dad's moves are so grand,
He's a confused penguin, you just don't understand.
Mom's laughter is music, so bright and so clear,
Joyful hearts around, let's toast with good cheer!

As stars twinkle down, like confetti on black,
We share silly secrets, then shove a snack.
In this warmth of our hearth, with family, we're blessed,
Joyful hearts all together, we could never be stressed.

The Melody of Us

When we sing our off-key, it's a glorious sound,
Like a herd of stampeding goats, close to the ground.
With spatulas wielded like swords in a fight,
The kitchen's our stage, our shows are a sight!

Baking a cake, but oops! There's a flop,
A sprinkle explosion—our sweet jaws just drop.
"Add more chocolate!" we shout with delight,
Creating a mess that'll last through the night.

The dog licks the floor, thinking it's grand,
While we dance like wildflowers, hand in hand.
Our laughter's the melody, sweet as can be,
In this funny little world, we feel totally free.

So here's to the chaos, the songs that we sing,
To the melody of us, oh, what joy it can bring!
With each silly moment, we're building a trust,
Strumming forever, the melody of us.

Candles Glow with Love's Embrace

Candles flicker gently, casting shadows that play,
A dance of the silly in an enchanting array.
With cake on the table, and frosting askew,
We sing happy faces and hope you'll join too!

Mom's wish is for peace, Dad wishes for snacks,
The cat wishes for fish, all curled by the racks.
We laugh as the candles lean ever so near,
One wish for the party, the laughter's so clear.

The stories come flying, like popcorn on edge,
"Remember that time?" we shout from the ledge.
In the glow of the flames, with love all around,
We savor each moment, happiness found.

So puff out the candles, let laughter ignite,
In this strange little place, our hearts feel so light.
As the night slips away with the stars shining bright,
Candles glow with love's embrace, oh, what a sight!

The Spirit of Giving Hearts

In a world of socks and ties,
The gift of laughter truly flies.
Unwrap the joy, the fun, the cheer,
For giving hearts bring love so near.

Cookies baked with extra sprinkles,
A gift that makes the tongue do twinkles.
Wrapped in smiles, a little dance,
The gift of joy is not by chance!

A yawn, a smile, my cat's new hat,
Who knew giving could be that flat?
Yet laughter's gold, it's pure and bright,
The spirit of giving is the light!

So share your hearts with silly hats,
A gift of joy that simply chats.
For in the laughter, hugs, and fun,
The spirit of giving's second to none!

Glowing Embers of Affection

In the fireplace, the marshmallows roast,
Oh, the gooey goodness we love most!
With chocolate rivers and graham's crisp,
S'mores of affection, can't resist!

The fire's glow plays tricks on the munch,
Who would dare have popcorn for lunch?
But warmth and giggles fill the air,
Our hearts ignited without a care.

With each crackle, our hearts ignite,
In bonfire nights, stories take flight.
The glowing embers dance with glee,
A spark of friendship, wild and free!

So gather 'round, share tales and cheer,
With silly jokes, and hearts sincere.
For in these moments, fiery and bright,
Our glowing love shines into the night!

A Tapestry of Smiles and Cheer

Stitching smiles from threads of gold,
Laughter woven, tales retold.
Each colorful patch a memory bright,
A tapestry of joy, pure delight!

With every giggle, a new design,
Woven together, hearts align.
A quirky patch, a funny face,
In this crazy quilt, we find our place!

When raindrops fall and skies turn grey,
Our smiles shine through, come what may.
In patches of kindness, we do create,
A cheerful fabric, love's true fate!

So gather your thread, and let's begin,
To weave a world where joy won't thin.
Through every stitch, let laughter steer,
A tapestry of smiles and cheer!

Starry Nights and Swaying Trees

Under starry skies, the trees do sway,
Whispering secrets of the day.
With crickets chirping their serenade,
A nighttime dance the world has made.

The moon winks down, a cheeky grin,
While sleepy owls start to spin.
The shadows play, a funny game,
Each rustling leaf whispers a name.

A bear in pajamas might stroll by,
A drowsy deer catches a sigh.
Fireflies twinkle in tiny streams,
Igniting laughter, fueling dreams!

So as we gaze, let's share a tease,
Imagine a world where giggles freeze.
In the cool night air, let worries cease,
With starry nights and swaying trees!

Chestnuts Roasting and Memories Made

Chestnuts roasting on a fire,
The smell is strong, it does inspire.
But wait, what's that, a squirrel's dare?
He's planning on stealing my warm fare.

Family gatherings lead to cheer,
But Uncle Joe always brings a beer.
He tells the tales, a bit too bold,
About the snowman that turned to gold.

Grandma's cookies fill the air,
They're soft and sweet, beyond compare.
But watch out now, don't take the last,
Or face her wrath, oh what a blast!

So here's to warmth and laughter bright,
With memories made 'neath starry night.
For in this life, we all must seize,
The joy in moments, heartily, please!

Hummingbirds of Hope and Joy

Hummingbirds flit with a buzz,
Dancing in gardens, what a fuzz!
They sip sweet nectar, oh so quick,
While I stand still, just feeling sick.

They float like tiny gems of light,
So full of joy, a pure delight.
While I, the grounded, hold my gin,
And wonder if I'll ever win.

Their wings a blur, a graceful sight,
I dream of soaring, taking flight.
But my flight's more like a lazy crawl,
As I forget where I left my shawl.

So here's to birds, so full of zest,
While I sit back and just take rest.
In hopes one day, I'll join their play,
And flutter through life in a better way!

Where Snow Falls Soft Like Dreams

Where snow falls soft like dreams at night,
I built a snowman, quite a sight.
But he melted fast—oh what a shock,
I thought he'd stay, like a big rock!

Snowball fights broke out with glee,
But then I slipped, oh what a spree!
Landed right in a snowdrift deep,
And all my friends just laughed and peeped.

Hot cocoa warming my cold hands,
With marshmallows that make life grand.
But don't you dare, touch my sweet mug,
Or feel the wrath of my playful bug!

So here's to winters, cold and bright,
With memories made in soft moonlight.
For joy is found, even in falls,
When snowflakes dance and laughter calls!

The Resonance of Love's Melody

In a quiet room, love's sweet song,
Where hearts beat loud, we both belong.
A serenade plays, oh so sweet,
But watch your step, or trip on your feet!

I sing off-key with all my might,
While you just giggle, what a sight.
But what's a tune without a laugh?
A recipe for a wobbly half!

We dance around without a care,
But then you pause, oh, it's not fair!
You step on my toes, and I squeal loud,
While the cat watches me, oh so proud.

So here's to love in all its forms,
With silly moments and quirky norms.
For in this melody, we'll always sway,
Creating memories that hope will stay!

Radiating Love in the Frosty Air

The snowflakes fall, a chilly sight,
But love keeps us warm, oh what a delight.
With mittens snug and hats pulled tight,
We giggle and dance, hearts feeling light.

Hot cocoa spills, a marshmallow mess,
You laugh so hard, I must confess.
Your nose is pink, your cheeks a flare,
In this frosty air, we joyfully share.

We build a snowman, a wobbly chap,
He wears your scarf, a funky wrap.
With carrot nose and a smile so wide,
Our wintry love feels like a joyride.

Under the moon, our warmth is clear,
Who needs the sun when I have you near?
This frosty air, with love it's rife,
A snow globe moment, our silly life.

Merry Melodies and Peaceful Echoes

The bells ring out with a merry chime,
Each note a laugh, each tune a rhyme.
We dance around in a wacky spin,
Your two left feet, my cheeky grin.

The turkey's burnt, oh what a sight,
We toast with soda, it feels just right.
With family tales and smiles so wide,
We cherish the chaos, our hearts collide.

Carols falter, forgotten words,
We sing like frogs, it's quite absurd.
Laughter echoes, fills the night,
In our merry mess, everything's bright.

So here's to joy and silly cheer,
To joyful noise that we hold dear.
In this sweet chaos, we find our way,
Merry melodies brighten our day.

The Tingle of Sweet Memories

Remember that time with the pie gone wrong?
We laughed till it hurt, couldn't help but prolong.
The filling shot out like a rocket in flight,
Your shocked little face was a glorious sight.

Or how about that sweater you tried to hide?
With cats on it dancing and a mismatched side?
We rocked that event like stars on a stage,
Laughing so hard, we forgot our age.

The silly debates over who made the best,
The world's worst joke still cracks us, no jest.
In the treasure chest of moments we claim,
Each giggle and snort is fueled by the same.

So here's to the memories, sweet and divine,
Each cringe and each chuckle, perfectly fine.
Through laughter we cherish what life does send,
In this merry tingle, the fun never ends.

A Warm Embrace Beneath the Stars

Under the blanket of twinkling glow,
We sip hot cocoa, just taking it slow.
You shiver and giggle, say, "It's too cold!"
Yet still you snuggle, a sight to behold.

The stars are the backdrop, a glimmering show,
Each wish we whisper, out into the flow.
You drop your marshmallows right in the drink,
We laugh at the splash, it's just what we think.

The night wears on, with stories we weave,
Jokes in the moonlight, no chance to grieve.
Wrapped tight together, we share goofy dreams,
In our world of wonders, nothing's as it seems.

So here's to the magic, the warmth we embrace,
Two silly souls in their silly place.
Beneath the stars, our laughter does soar,
In this cozy moment, who could ask for more?

A Garland of Sweet Memories

In grandma's kitchen, pies set high,
The cat sneezes, oh my, oh my!
With flour on noses, we bake and giggle,
Our sweet little secrets, a dance, a wiggle.

A trip to the park, swing sets galore,
Fell off a slide, then back for more!
Ice cream cones melting in sun's golden rays,
Chasing my brother through long summer days.

Each birthday candle, wishes so grand,
With a cake that's too big for one small hand.
Ice cream wars lead to giggles and mess,
Still, we clean up, we couldn't care less!

In every laugh, a memory thrives,
In the garden of love, our joy still survives.
Each moment a flower, each smile a cheer,
In our garland of memories, forever we'll steer.

Twinkling Eyes and Tender Smiles

Your twinkling eyes like stars that glow,
With tender smiles, they steal the show.
A wink here and there, what mischief you'll spark,
Like a playful puppy chasing the dark.

In silly hats and mismatched socks,
You dance around, oh how time talks!
With giggling toddlers and your funny frown,
You lift us up when we feel down.

The twirl of joy when the music plays,
We snicker and joke in the craziest ways.
Do you recall our leapfrog dreams?
With twinkling eyes, we burst at the seams!

Tender smiles are gifts that truly inspire,
With each silly prank, our hearts catch fire.
In this quirky world, together we'll roam,
With laughter our anchor, forever our home.

The Spirit of Giving in the Air

The spirit of giving floats like a kite,
Wrapping all hearts in warmth and delight.
With cookies we bake, and gifts we bestow,
Even socks for Grandpa, just to see him glow.

We sing silly songs, off-key but loud,
Making the shyest, so very proud.
A hug here, a smile there, cheer all around,
In the spirit of giving, love knows no bound.

With bright wrapping paper that's crinkled and torn,
We dance in the chaos of this joyful morn.
Each clumsy attempt at a festive surprise,
Creates joyful laughter with bright, shiny eyes.

So here's to the silliness, loud and divine,
In this season of giving, oh how we shine!
With hearts full of joy and laughter that sings,
The spirit of giving makes our heartstrings.

Echoes of Cheer in the Frosted Air

In frosted air, echoes of cheer,
Above us, snowflakes twirl without fear.
We build a snowman, a hat oh so bright,
He promptly falls over, what a funny sight!

With laughter and warmth in every gust,
A snowball fight! Who's winning? We trust!
In mittens and scarves, all bundled tight,
We twirl down the hill, what a playful flight!

The cocoa we sip is steaming and sweet,
With marshmallows floating, a fluffy treat.
And when we spill it, we laugh and we cheer,
For moments like these, we all hold so dear.

With echoes of joy, the season unfolds,
Through frosted air, every memory holds.
Together we gather, in warmth we confer,
In the dance of the winter, hearts start to stir.

When Hearts Collide in Joy

Two hearts collide with goofy grins,
Like bumper cars, where laughter begins.
We trip on love, like it's a game,
And giggle loudly, forgetting our shame.

A wink, a smile, we're both so bold,
Like dancing clowns, our story unfolds.
Jokes fly high, we snort like pigs,
In this circus of love, we dance our jig.

Ice cream spills and pizza fights,
Love's not perfect, but oh, what delights!
We wear mismatched socks just for fun,
In this crazy world, we are the one.

So let's collide, let's make a mess,
In the chaos, we find our best.
With hearts so full, we laugh and sigh,
Love's a ride, come jump, oh my!

A Fireside Winter's Serenade

By the fire, we roast our toes,
Singing tunes that nobody knows.
Hot cocoa spills, oh what a sight,
With marshmallow ghosts dancing at night.

We're wrapped in blankets, cozy tight,
While snowflakes fall, pure and white.
We share old jokes and clumsy dance,
Fireside romance, oh what a chance!

The dog joins in, a furry mound,
As we trip over the logs we found.
Our laughter rings, a merry tune,
While outside howls the winter moon.

In this frosty, glowing embrace,
We're on a love adventure, what a race!
With hearts ablaze and spirits high,
By the fire, we dream and fly.

Frosty Windows and Love's Touch

Frosty windows, breath makes art,
We scribble hearts, it's a true fine start.
Wrapped in scarves, we warm each other,
Love's a blanket, cozy like a mother.

Outside's a tundra, inside's a dance,
We twirl and slip in a silly prance.
The heater's on, but we bring the heat,
Two frozen snowmen, oh what a feat!

Hot tea spills as we laugh and play,
While winter whispers, "Stay, oh stay!"
Through misty panes our giggles flow,
In this frosty world, love's all aglow.

So here we are, two playful fools,
Ignoring the cold, just breaking the rules.
With frosty windows and warm hearts,
In this crazy winter, love never departs.

Evergreen Memories and Bright Dreams

Under the tree, we make our plans,
With silly hats and funny fans.
We wrap ourselves in tinsel glory,
Creating a holiday of awkward story.

Pine scents linger, we bake and spill,
Sugar cookies give us a thrill.
We laugh at mishaps, oh what a scene,
In this evergreen dream, we're both the Queen.

Twinkling lights hang with flair,
While we dance like we just don't care.
We build a fort of soft green bliss,
In this madness, who'd want to miss?

So here's to us, on this bright night,
With evergreen memories shining so bright.
Laughter and love make every theme,
In our wonderful, wild, bright dream.

Adventures in a Winter Wonderland

In a snowball fight, I took my aim,
But I slipped and fell, oh what a shame!
The snowman chuckled, his nose a carrot,
While I lay there, feeling like a parrot.

Skiing down hills, I'm feeling so bold,
But backwards I go, as my friends unfold.
Riding on ice, it's a slippery dance,
I twirl and I spin, it's a comic romance.

Hot cocoa spills, I'm wearing a smile,
Marshmallows bounce, they travel a mile.
Building a fort, my fort's quite the sight,
Yet snowflakes land right; now I'm in a plight.

So here's to the joy, of winter's embrace,
With laughter and slips, we find our own place.
In winter wonder, we find our cheer,
Together we play, throughout the whole year.

Serenade of the Season's Heart

The carolers sing with a twist and a cheer,
Their notes go off-key, yet we all persevere.
With cocoa in hand, we sway to the beat,
We laugh at the cold, as we dance on our feet.

Cookies are baking, but oh what a mess,
Flour on my face is my own kind of dress.
I aimed for the oven, but landed too wide,
Now I'm stuck in the dough, on a delicious ride.

Gifts wrapped in paper, with bows gone awry,
I taped my own fingers, I think I might cry!
Yet laughter erupts as I trip on the floor,
A season of joy, who could ask for more?

In this festive time, let's embrace all the fun,
With hearts feeling light, and our worries all done.
A serenade sweet, of the season's delight,
We sing through the chaos, and dance through the night.

Whispers of Winter's Embrace

Snowflakes are whispering, soft in the night,
They blanket the ground, all fluffy and white.
But slipping and sliding, my legs in a knot,
I'm flailing for balance, forgetting the plot.

A penguin I spotted on a chilly spree,
He waddled on by, and laughed right at me.
I tried to be graceful, I gave it a whirl,
But landed face-first in a snow-covered swirl.

Chili's on stovetop, oh what a great smell,
Yet somehow the cat thinks it's her new shell.
She jumps on the counter, a furry ballet,
Now we both have a story for winter's display.

Each hug of the cold is a giggle and cheer,
With friends all around, there's nothing to fear.
Whispers of winter, a magical trace,
In laughter we find, our warmest embrace.

The Heart's Festive Melody

Jingle bells jangle with a misfit sound,
As my cat grabs a ribbon and dances around.
He pounces and leaps, oh what a delight,
Soon tripping me up in the midst of the night.

Chopping the veggies, I swear I can sing,
But those onions lurking, they're a sneaky thing.
Tears start to flow, I'm a sight to behold,
With a knife in one hand, and a laugh uncontrolled.

The lights on the tree are a tangle of fun,
Each bulb tells a story, oh what have I done?
I swap red for green, then purple with gold,
Now it's a disco, with memories bold.

So here's to the laughter, the joy, and the cheer,
The heart's festive melody, ringing so clear.
With each little mishap, we grow ever fonder,
Together in magic, we joyfully wander.

Love's Warm Whisper in the Chill

In winter's frost, your nose is red,
You try to warm it with my head.
We laugh and snuggle, can't feel the cold,
Your heart's a treasure, more than gold.

We dance on ice, like penguins bold,
Trip and tumble, oh, if I could be told!
Hot cocoa spills, our mittens cling,
We giggle together, let the snowflakes sing.

Your mitts are gone, where could they be?
Why did I think those were for me?
With every hug, I feel the glow,
Love's warm whisper through the frosty glow.

So here we sit, the candles blink,
With funny faces, you make me think.
In every chill, you've got the spark,
Love's laughter echoes, lighting the dark.

An Evening Filled with Laughter

The clock strikes eight, the fun begins,
In our living room, laughter wins.
Jokes are flying, your punchlines zing,
I'm rolling on the floor, what a fling!

We play charades, I flail my arms,
You guess my silly, hilarious charms.
Your face turns red, it's quite a sight,
Like a tomato, but oh so bright!

The neighbors shout, 'Keep it down, you two!'
We wave and shout, 'We love you too!'
With every giggle, the night grows long,
Our hearts like music, spinning a song.

An evening filled with quirky glee,
In your laughter, I'm always free.
So let's keep laughing, what do you say?
Where humor lives, let us stay!

Candles, Cocoa, and Closeness

Candles flicker, shadows dance,
In this cozy spot, we take a chance.
Your smile bright, a sweet delight,
While sipping cocoa, oh what a night!

We tell ghost stories, your eyes go wide,
Then I fake a howl, it's hard to hide.
With every sip, we share our dreams,
In the rich cocoa, life's sweeter than creams.

You spill your drink, a chocolate sea,
I don't mind, come sit with me!
With blankets piled, we cozy in tight,
Your warmth wraps around, it feels so right.

As candles melt, they lead the way,
To sleepy giggles at the end of the day.
In this moment, forever stays,
With cocoa love, we're here to play!

The Magic of Shared Moments

Two cups clink, a secret toast,
To silly times we love the most.
We share a glance, and then we grin,
In these moments, we always win.

Strolling through parks, we chase the birds,
You make up poems, I mix the words.
We laugh so loud, our joy's the rhyme,
In every heartbeat, it feels like time.

Picnics gone wrong, the ants arrive,
You shriek and stand, we come alive!
A sandwich flies, a dance emerges,
In every mishap, laughter surges.

So here's to us, the silly and sweet,
With every smile, we can't be beat.
In shared moments, love starts to bloom,
Like flowers of laughter in every room.

Flickering Lights and Boundless Joy

In the dark, the bulbs start to blink,
A dance of chaos, do you think?
They flicker and pop, a merry show,
Yet, leave us in darkness, oh, woe!

The cat leaps high, like a little star,
Chasing shadows, oh dear, where are we ajar?
With each flip, I trip on my shoelace,
In this light circus, I'm losing my pace!

Festive cheer from lights on a spree,
Decorations sparkle, like glee in a tree.
But batteries die too quickly, oh what a plight,
It's a battle of bulbs every single night!

Yet laughter echoes, as we make do,
In this glowing chaos, joy shines through.
For in flickering lights, we find our glow,
Boundless joy even when bulbs won't show!

A Canvas of Love in the Winter

Snowflakes fall, like bits of fluff,
I try to catch them, but it's tough.
The cold makes my nose a rosy hue,
Yet, all I can think of is hot cocoa too!

Wrapped in scarves, we venture out,
Building snowmen, there's no doubt.
But he's a little lumpy, a bit bow-legged,
A masterpiece of winter, slightly misguided!

We draw hearts on the frosty glass,
Hoping the chill in the air won't last.
But as we stumble through drifts so deep,
Laughter echoes in a fond memory heap!

With every snowball, our giggles unfold,
A canvas of love as the chilly air holds.
In winter's embrace, we find what is true,
Warmth in our hearts, even with the blue!

Hearts Dancing to Silent Nights

Under stars, the world is still,
But my heart races, it's quite a thrill.
In silent nights, we sway with glee,
Like awkward dancers at a grand soiree!

Dreams pirouette on the moonlit stage,
Like a story that just won't age.
Our laughter fills the chilly air,
Moving together, a goofy pair!

Fanciful whispers float in the breeze,
As we step on toes and stumble with ease.
Each twirl brings giggles, a clumsy delight,
In silent nights, we dance until light!

So here we sway, in the cool of the dark,
Our own little world, where we spark.
With each beat of laughter, our hearts take flight,
Dancing together through silent nights!

Tuning into the Magic of Us

In the chaos of life, we find our tune,
Adjusting our dials, under the moon.
A melody made of laughter and fun,
Two hearts syncing like a catchy run!

With mismatched socks, and a sprinkle of flair,
Together we stumble without a care.
The rhythm of love, sometimes offbeat,
Yet, in our harmony, life feels sweet!

We waltz through the kitchen, dance on the floor,
Spinning with joy, and sometimes a snore.
But every note is a colorful blast,
In the symphony of us, we're unsurpassed!

So here's to the magic, the laughter, the fuss,
Tuning into the moments that make us, us.
In the playlist of life, let's sing it loud,
For in our duet, I couldn't be prouder!

Symphony of the Season's Delight

Snowflakes dance, they twirl and spin,
Cats chase tails, while we just grin.
Hot cocoa spills, on my new coat,
Life's a joke, on this old boat.

Twinkling lights, they blink and glow,
Frosty breath, like clouds in tow.
The carols play, off-key yet loud,
We sing along, oh, aren't we proud?

Cookies burn, as we laugh and shout,
Silly mistakes, that's what it's about.
Gifts wrapped tight, in paper and bows,
What's inside? Nobody knows!

From winter's chill, we find our heat,
Gathered 'round, with sugary treat,
Laughter rings, in joyful cheer,
In this season, we hold dear.

Joyful Echoes in Frosted Air

Snowmen wobble, with carrot nose,
They tip and fall, oh dear, who knows?
Sledding down hills, we crash and roll,
Winter's laugh, it takes its toll.

Frosty mornings, we sip our brew,
Slippers on feet, it's a cozy view.
Yet in the fridge, we've lost some bread,
Who ate it last? Let's place our bets!

Chasing snowflakes, with hands out wide,
Oh, what fun, in this frosty ride!
We build a fort, then throw some snow,
Battle begins — we're high, then low.

Echoing joy, with every laugh,
Mom lost her shoe, and Dad's in half!
In this season, we love to share,
Joyful echoes, fill the air.

Carols of the Heart's Desire

Jingle bells ring, we sing off-key,
Dancing along, a sight to see!
Empty glasses, oops, did I break?
Singing louder, for goodness' sake!

Socks on our hands, it's a brand new trend,
Stumbling through tunes, we just pretend.
Elves in the corner, they laugh and sway,
What's on the menu? Just cookies today!

Mistletoe hung, with care and flair,
Someone just slipped, oh well, beware!
Twinkling eyes, with hopes and dreams,
In this season, we burst at the seams!

Carols of joy, our hearts' delight,
Together we sing, we'll be up all night.
With every note, finds its way,
What a wild, magical day!

Together in the Cozy Glow

Fireplace crackles, sipping warm cheer,
Blankets are flying, with laughter near.
Chasing the shadows, we wiggle and tease,
Handmade gifts, crafted with ease.

Pajamas adorned, we strut like pros,
Home alone movies, we'll never close.
Popcorn spills, it covers the floor,
Who needs decor? We have galore!

With cookies half-baked, and stories to share,
Our hearts are full, with love in the air.
Chasing each other, through rooms bright and warm,
Together we stand, through any storm.

In this cozy glow, we find our delight,
Endless laughter, well into the night.
Whatever may come, we laugh and we play,
Together forever, in our own way.

Milton Keynes UK
Ingram Content Group UK Ltd.
UKHW010227111224
452348UK00011B/571